Totem Poles and Tribes

by Nancy Lyon

A
cpi
Book

From

RAINTREE CHILDRENS BOOKS
Milwaukee • Toronto • Melbourne • London

Copyright© 1977 by Contemporary Perspectives, Inc.
All rights reserved. No part of this book may be reproduced or utilized in any form
or by any means, electronic or mechanical, including photocopying, recording, or
by any information storage and retrieval system, without permission in writing from
the Distributor and the Publisher. Inquiries should be addressed to the
DISTRIBUTOR: Raintree Publishers Limited, 205 West Highland Avenue,
Milwaukee, Wisconsin 53203 and the PUBLISHER: Contemporary Perspectives,
Inc., Suite 6A, 230 East 48th Street, New York, New York 10017.

Library of Congress Number: 77-23748

Art and Photo Credits

Cover photo, National Parks Service.
Photo on page 8, Steve Wilson/dpi
Photo on page 13, Ward Wells/dpi
Illustrations on pages 17, 30, 32, and 41, Connie Maltese.
Photos on pages 19 and 23, S. J. Krasemann, National Audubon Society/Photo
Researchers, Inc.
Photo on page 21, Paolo Koch/Photo Researchers, Inc.
Photos on pages 27, 34, 36, and 47, Museum of the American Indian, Heye
Foundation.
Illustrations on pages 29 and 39, and photo on page 44, New York Public Library
Picture Collection.
Photo on page 31, Floyd Norgaard/dpi.
Photo on page 35, Beinecke Rare Book and Manuscript Library, Yale University.
All photo research for this book was provided by Roberta Guerette.
Every effort has been made to trace the ownership of all copyrighted material in this
book and to obtain permission for its use.

Library of Congress Cataloging in Publication Data

Lyon, Nancy.
  Totem poles and tribes.

  SUMMARY: A history of totem poles and a discussion of the tribes that used
them. Includes some stories told on these tall wood columns.
    1. Indians of North America—Northwest coast of North
America—Juvenile literature. 2. Totem poles—Juvenile literature.
[1. Indians of North America—Northwest coast of North
America. 2. Totem Poles. 3. Indians of North America—Northwest
coast of North America—Legends] I. Title.
E78.N78L96   970'.004'97   77-23748
ISBN 0-8172-1044-X lib. bdg.

Manufactured in the United States of America.
ISBN 0-8172-1044-X

Contents

Animal Magic

Chapter 1

Most Indians knew that it was not wise to make fun of animals. But there were some who forgot at times. There were others who didn't believe in animals' magic. For such a sin, non-believers would pay dearly—often with their very lives. Animals could work all sorts of magic. Usually, they used their magic to help people in trouble. But when they were angry, they could bring torture, pain, and horrible death. The animals could even change themselves into human beings or into other animals and then change back again.

5

No, a wise Indian knew better than to poke fun at nature's creatures. But there is an old Indian tale that one day, in a certain village, a certain chief's daughter made a certain mistake. *She laughed at a frog!*

Later that evening, the chief's daughter went for a walk. A handsome young man suddenly appeared and asked her to marry him. She looked at his shining eyes, listened to his soft, deep voice, and knew she loved him. Many young men had wanted to marry her, but she did not like any of them. The chief's daughter wanted to marry *this* young man.

He asked her to his father's house. Pointing to the lake, he said the house was nearby. When they reached the house, a door opened for them. But the young woman saw that it was not a door at all. It was really an edge of the lake that had lifted up! They went under and she met many more young people there.

Meanwhile, the chief worried about his daughter. She had disappeared! Friends and relatives looked for her everywhere but could not find her. Finally, they thought she must be dead, and they gave up the search. A year passed. All hope of finding the young woman was gone.

Then, one day in the spring, an Indian boy saw the chief's daughter. She was sitting among a group of frogs. They were sunning themselves on a rock in the lake. The boy ran back to the village and shouted the news. The chief and all his family ran to the lake with many valuable gifts to persuade the frog tribe to let the girl go. The chief begged to have his daughter back, but the frogs refused to let her leave. The chief became angry and ordered his tribe to drain the lake.

The Indians dug a trench to let the water flow out of the lake. The frogs hopped away in all directions. But the chief's daughter clung to a log and floated to the edge of the lake. When the chief pulled his daughter from the water, he saw that she had the skin of a frog.

She was taken home and slowly became human again. But her problems were far from over. The girl who had once laughed at a frog found she could no longer eat human food. She soon died.

This story is thousands of years old. It is one of hundreds of Indian tales of myth, magic, and superstition. The Indians feared the magical powers of the animals around them. When

Totem poles tell strange stories of magic and superstition.

strangers would come to their villages, Indians thought they might be animals in disguise. They believed these magical creatures could lure them to remote places and punish them for wrongdoings.

How do we know this story? This Indian myth and hundreds more appear on *totem poles*. Totem poles reveal much about Indian super-stition, life, and legend. Totems are really the unwritten language of the old Indian world. Let's travel through that world for a little while.

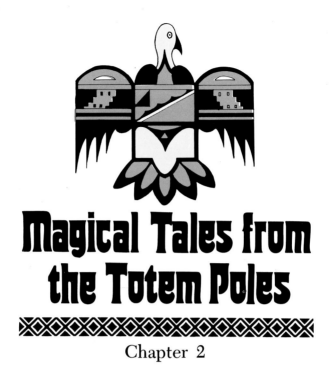

Magical Tales from the Totem Poles

XXXXXXXXXXXXXXXXXXXXXXXXX

Chapter 2

To the Indians, all living things had magical powers that could help or harm them. Not a blackberry was picked, not a fish was caught, not a tree was carved before it was honored with a prayer of thanks.

The totem stories answered questions about the magic of the natural world. *What caused thunder?* The totems answered:

It was a huge bird, the Thunderbird, who lived high in the mountains. Its body was so big that, when it

flew to get its food, it darkened
the entire sky. The flapping of
its giant wings made the thunder.

No question was too hard for the totems to
answer. They told of everything in the Indians'
world. *Where did the first mosquitoes come
from?* The Indians read the magical answer from
the totem pole:

A giant cannibal once fed upon the
Indians. He was feared for years,
until finally he was caught and
quickly burned to death. So angry
was the awful cannibal that from his
ashes rose pesky insects that, to this
day, go on "eating people."

The Indians loved stories of brave and
clever adventurers. The heroes of these stories
were often animals. *Raven* was one of their most
popular characters. The Indians believed that
the all-black raven was once an all-*white* bird.
The white-feathered Raven was a trickster who
had the power to change himself into anything
he wished. Here is a story from the totem pole
that tells how the sun, moon, and stars came into
the world.

RAVEN AND THE
EVIL MAGICIAN

The Sun was kept hidden in a box in the house of an evil magician. Raven knew this and wanted to free the Sun. He went to the house where the Sun was kept and saw that the magician's daughter always went to the same stream to drink. Raven changed himself into a hemlock needle and floated into her cup.

But the girl knew about Raven and his tricks. Something told her the hemlock needle might be Raven. She would not drink the water. Raven was very upset! He turned himself into a grain of sand, so tiny that she couldn't see it. She drank the water and Raven with it!

Once inside the girl's body, Raven took the form of a human baby. Many months later, the magician's daughter gave birth to a little boy. She did not know her new baby boy was really Raven. The new baby would cry and cry. No matter what toy they brought him he was un-happy. He wanted only what was in the box. Finally, his grandfather gave in. He took out the Sun to let the new baby play with it. *Raven had won—he had the Sun!*

The bird was a popular figure on totem poles.

13

Quickly changing back into his bird form, Raven flew up the smokehole of the house, holding the Sun very tightly. The magician was angry and made the flames of his fire leap up to burn Raven. Raven escaped the flames, but they scorched him and turned his white coat of feathers black. Since then, all ravens have been black.

The magician did not give up easily. Using his magic powers, he flew after Raven. Raven soon got tired because the Sun was heavy. But the magician was gaining on him. To lighten the weight of his load, Raven broke off a few pieces of the Sun. He threw them into the sky where they became stars.

Once more the magician was catching up with him. Again, Raven broke off another chunk of the Sun and threw it into the sky. That became the moon. Finally, the tired Raven threw the rest of the Sun up into the sky where it has shone ever since.

This story of Raven was as familiar to the Indians as *Jack and the Beanstalk* or *Little Red Riding Hood* are to us. There are hundreds of other totem pole stories involving Raven, many of them less well-known. Each appeared on the totem poles of the family who "owned" the story.

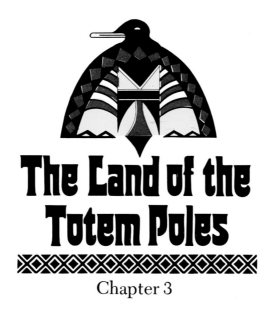

The Land of the Totem Poles

XXXXXXXXXXXXXXXXX

Chapter 3

Along the Pacific Coast of North America, from southern Alaska to southern British Columbia, there is an historical record not found anywhere else in the world. This is the land of winter fog and rain. It is a land of sweet smelling cedar trees. It is also the land where many tribes of Indians lived for more years than any other Americans can imagine.

In this land lived tribes whose names most of us don't know—the Tlingkits (TLING-kits), the Kwakiutl (Kwak-YOU-tul), the Haida (HIGH-duh), and many more. While these names may not mean very much to us today, these Northwest Indians left hundreds of magical stories that are

15

still being read. They did this without ever writing a word.

The Northwest tribes told the modern world their stories through the language of their totem poles. These beautiful columns of wood are carved from tall cedar trees. The totems picture the birds, fish, animals, humans, and strange creatures from the world of Indian legend. The carved figures look down and laugh at us. But sometimes they also tell us stories of the people who made them.

Nobody knows why, in all the world, totem poles are found only here. But the stories of who carved the poles, how and when the art of carving began, and why the tribes stopped carving them, tell us much more about the Indians than any history book.

For example, a totem pole of the Haida tribe tells the following story about how the Indians learned to carve wood.

One winter day a man called Master Carver came to the village. He was oddly dressed in a carved, painted headdress and a goat-wool shirt with many designs on it. The strangest thing about Master Carver, though, was that his body

Totem pole carvers were honored members of the community.

was covered with tattoos. His skin was a picture story. Even his fingernails were painted with drawings of human faces.

The villagers, of course, found him very interesting. They listened when he told them, "Something will happen during the night. Go to bed. Don't pay attention to anything that you hear. Don't stir until morning, when you are sure the sun is up."

In the morning they were amazed. The roof-posts of their houses had been carved. All

17

the walls had been painted with human and animal figures. In front of each house were three carved and painted poles. The Indians had never seen anything like them!

The Haidas wanted to copy what they saw. Master Carver was only too glad to instruct them. Each day he explained the meaning of a different face. Then he would carve the face in wood. That way, the Haidas learned the secrets of carving.

The Indians often used stories of magic to explain how things came to be. In this story, Master Carver clearly had to be a magician to carve all those faces in one night.

The Indians didn't write down their history, so no one knows when totem pole carving began. We can't even tell from the age of poles that have been found. In the damp, foggy climate of the Pacific Northwest, wood objects don't last long. Many of the old totem poles rotted away. Today, there aren't many totem poles left that are more than 100 years old.

We know that the use of totem poles is much, much older than a mere 100 years! When the first Europeans came to the Northwest in the late 1700s, they found totem poles. The famous Captain Cook wrote of the carved poles he saw in

1778. Later, in 1791, a Frenchman named Marchand wrote about the doorway to one Haida house he saw. The housefront was a single piece of wood cut from the trunk of a great tree, and the doorway looked like a huge, open mouth.

Marchand told of the carvings on it—frogs, toads, lizards and other animals, and humans.

This colorful totem covers a ceremonial house in Alaska.

Although we may never know when totem art began, there is much we do know about totem poles. We have learned, for example, that totem poles were *not* Indian idols, as the first European explorers thought. Totem poles were carved as family *emblems*. The emblem for one family group might be an eagle. The emblem for another might be a raven, or a wolf, or a bear.

Most totems also told bits of stories. The Indians believed their ancestors were animals who had become people, and the animal totems told a "family history." If you could "read" the totem poles, you could put together wonderful stories from their carved figures.

Totems told stories of birds who had come to earth. These birds took off their masks and feathers to become people. The poles told of sea and land creatures who had changed their animal shapes to take on human forms.

All around the Indian houses stood these beautiful carved poles with their magical family stories. A totem pole 70 feet high might stand in the front of the house. Inside the house, totem poles stood as tall as 12 feet. Totems for the dead were carved on *memorial* poles that were put in front of the house or at the family burial grounds.

This memorial totem belonged to the Kwakiutl Indians.

Indians also used totem poles to mark property they owned. Such a pole might be thought of as a sign that tells others, "This property belongs to . . . . " To protect a rich salmon stream, a Northwest Indian might have put up his family totem poles along the stream banks. Another pole might be put up as a public record of a debt one family might have to another.

But when we think of totem poles today, we are most drawn to the exciting and magical stories they tell. In the totems carved by a Haida chief, there is still another story of Raven and his adventures. Whether the chief's ancestors had told the story or whether he simply "bought" it from

21

someone is not known. But since it is told on *his* totem pole, it is considered to be *his* story. And a good story it is!

RAVEN, FOG WOMAN, AND THE FIRST SALMON

One day Raven was fishing from a canoe. He had two slaves with him. Raven caught only "bullheads," spiny fish that were something like catfish. Disappointed, Raven and the two slaves paddled back to camp. On the way, they became lost in a heavy fog. Suddenly, a woman appeared and sat down in their canoe. *How had this woman gotten into Raven's boat?*

Softly, the woman asked Raven for his hat. She held it up and caught all the fog in it. Because the sun shone again, they were able to find their way back to camp. Raven couldn't believe what had happened! He and Fog Woman fell in love and got married.

Later, Raven went on another fishing trip and took one slave—Gitsaqeq—with him. The other slave—Gitsanuk—stayed in camp with Fog

Salmon were
important fish to
the Indians. They
often appeared on
totem poles.

Woman. While Raven was away, his wife and the slave became hungry. Fog Woman ordered Gitsanuk to fetch a bucket of water. She dipped a finger into the water. Then she told the slave to face in the direction of the sea and to pour the water into a pool. Gitsanuk did and was surprised to find a large sockeye salmon in the pool.

The slave cooked the fish and the two ate a big meal. Fog Woman told Gitsanuk to clean the fish from his teeth. She didn't want Raven to see that they had eaten a new and delicious kind of fish without him. She also told the slave not to say a word about this to Raven, no matter what.

Either the slave didn't do a very good cleaning job, or Raven was more clever than Fog Woman thought. When he came back, Raven said he noticed a tiny piece of fish still caught between Gitsanuk's teeth. He angrily asked Gitsanuk about it. The frightened slave lied, saying it was only the flesh of bullheads. Raven became even angrier because he did not believe Gitsanuk. Finally Raven frightened the slave into telling him what had happened.

Raven then asked his wife to show proof of her secret powers. She had him fill his hat with water. She dipped four fingers into it. Amazingly, four salmon flopped onto the ground when he poured out the water.

Raven stared in wonder. He had never seen such fish as these salmon! After eating a fine dinner, Raven wondered if his wife could produce more. Fog Woman told Raven to bring her a bowl of water. She then washed her head in the water he brought. She asked Raven to empty the water back into the spring from which he had taken it. Instantly, the spring was filled with salmon!

Raven built a smokehouse to dry the fish. It was soon filled to the roof with salmon. He was so excited that he began to talk rudely to his wife, ordering her to make more and more fish. They argued. Suddenly, Raven lost control of himself and struck her. She told him that she would leave him, but still he continued to talk badly to her. Fog Woman cried and brushed her hair wildly.

A strange sound, like a rush of wind, came from the smokehouse. Fog Woman left the house and went down to the water. The sound from the smokehouse grew louder and louder. Raven saw that she was really leaving and tried to grab her, but he failed. She slipped, as the fog would, right through his hands.

As Fog Woman disappeared into the sea, all the salmon followed her. Soon, she and the fish were gone. Raven told his slaves not to worry. "We still have fish in the smokehouse for the winter," he said. He didn't know that they were gone too. Only a few bullheads were left.

But the salmon return to the Indian streams every year. Fog Woman and her daughter, Creek Woman, live at the head of the streams and bring the salmon back.

The Indians believed in fighting magic with magic. Even though he was blessed with strong magical powers, Raven was not always the winner in his fights with other magical creatures, such as Fog Woman.

Would you like to know how the totem figures look on the pole that told the Fog Woman story? High on the pole is the owner's emblem—the figure of a mythical bird called the *Kadjuk*. That bird lived high in the mountains. It was brown with black-tipped wings. Underneath the emblem there is a blank space on the pole.

The blank represents the high altitude where the Kadjuk lived. Below the empty space, the story figures appear. First there are two bird

The Raven even appeared on wooden rattles.

figures, side by side. These are Gitsanuk and Gitsaqeq, Raven's two slaves. Below them is Raven himself. Fog Woman appears next holding two salmon.

The Totem Tribes

What did totem poles mean to the Indians of the Northwest? Who carved them? When were they carved and why did the tribes stop carving them?

The Northwest tribes were sometimes called "Salmon and Cedar People." Salmon was their most important food. Cedar was their most important building material. The Indians were fishermen and expert woodworkers. These tribes were fortunate. Their land was rich and abundant. It provided them with everything they needed.

Summer was the time for fishing. Whole families would move to the fishing grounds to "harvest the crop" from the waters. The tribes developed ways of drying, smoking, and storing fish so that the catch would serve as a food supply for the whole year round.

With the basic food supply stored for the year, the winter was like a vacation. Days would be spent leisurely mending tools or fishing equipment. There was time to relax. There was also plenty of time for ceremonies and feasting.

The Northwest tribes had a rich cultural life. They sang and acted and danced their stories. Their celebrations were colorful and mysterious.

Indian life centered around fishing, hunting, and carving totems.

Spirits of the dead might speak from the fire. (Actually, an actor hidden in a hole in the floor spoke through a tube made from a sea plant.) *Strange creatures would fly through the air.* (These were puppets worked by men hidden in the rafters.) Sometimes *one creature would even change into another right before the eyes of the audience.* (This was done with a hinged wooden mask that had two faces carved on it.)

The Indian dance ceremony was performed to speak to the dead.

The Indians believed animals had magical powers.

During the free time of the winter months, the wood carver could practice his art. His first carved objects were probably small and simple. They were spoons, dolls, and wooden chests.

Beaver

Killer Whale

Mountain
Goat

Eagle

Grizzly
Bear

Each animal carving had a specific trademark.

Masks most likely came later and, finally, the totem poles.

The totems show the strange and powerful beauty of Indian carving. Many figures are of real animals made to look fantastic. Is that because the Indians thought animals were magical? Or was it, perhaps, simply a matter of space?

The totem pole designers had to fit many, many figures onto a pole. Characters would be squeezed, hunched, and squashed. They were placed one on top of the other, without room for their full bodies.

How did the Indians know one figure from another if they didn't look realistic? It was even difficult to tell the humans from the animals! But each carving had special features that identified it. The raven always had a straight beak, while the eagle's beak was curved. The hawk's beak curved around to touch its face. The beaver had buckteeth and a stick to chew on. The bear and wolf at first seemed difficult to tell apart. But the Indians would always know each by its ears. Bear ears stood straight up, while wolf ears slanted back.

Over and over, the totem poles told stories of magic and superstition. One pole found in the Haida village of Skedans, British Columbia, tells another Raven story. At the bottom of the pole is the figure of a great chief called *Qingi*. Raven and Qingi have had an argument over something.

Raven, whom we know is easily angered, decides to punish the chief. He causes a flood in Qingi's village. But Qingi has his own magical powers and saves his people from drowning, using nothing more than his *hat*!

These three totems were carved in a Haida village.

Of course, a hat belonging to a magical chief wouldn't be just an everyday kind of hat. Qingi could make his hat grow whenever he wished. When Raven sent the waters to flood the village, Qingi's hat kept getting bigger and bigger. The totem pole shows the villagers climbing up Qingi's hat to escape the flood waters.

At the top of the totem pole is an eagle. We know that the Northwest Indians formed family groups, called *clans*. We also know that the *Eagle Clan* was probably a wealthy family group. Not just anybody could have a totem pole carved. The pole carvers were very well paid. To have their own totem pole, a family had to have wealth.

The family could not simply put anything it wanted on a totem pole. The crest, and whatever else was carved on the pole, had to *belong* to the particular family. The family could win their crest

The potlatch gift-giving ceremony was an important custom.

by marrying, by buying it, or by receiving it as a gift. The family could even win it in war. By killing an enemy, a man had the right to display the enemy's crests and use his stories.

The celebration of the new totem pole was usually a big one, with many gifts given. The parties were called *potlatches*, which comes from an Indian word meaning "gift." The host family would give gifts to all the guests who came.

Blankets were a favorite gift, for the value of things was often counted in blankets. Canoes, tools, jewelry, chests, clothing, weapons—even slaves—might be given as gifts at a potlatch.

This mechanical halibut was used in a potlatch ceremony.

At the potlatch, the host could demonstrate how wealthy he was. The more gifts he gave away, the higher he would be ranked in the tribe.

Does it seem foolish to give away all this hard-earned wealth? Actually, *it wasn't being given away at all.* The guests were expected to hold their own potlatches and give back something of greater value. So these potlatch gifts were more like loans.

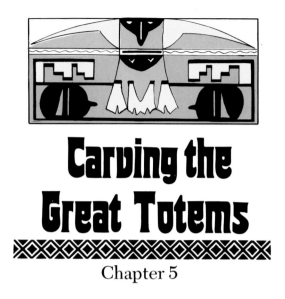

Carving the Great Totems

Even if we can't be sure when the first totem poles were carved, we have a good idea of *how* they were carved. Before the Indians learned of metal, they made carving tools from stone, bone, jade, and even beaver teeth! They would cut down the red cedar trees with stone axes. Then they would scoop out wood and shape the tree's surface with a tool called an *adze*. This was a sharp tool with a bone or shell blade at a right angle to the handle. If the wood surface was too rough after the use of the adze and bone chisels, the Indians smoothed it with stones. They finished it with their own form of "sandpaper"—the skin of a shark.

The Indians used mixtures of fungus, moss, berries, and different vegetables to color their totem poles. The colors were simple and the Indians didn't paint the poles heavily. They would never cover an entire totem pole with paint but just outline the carvings.

Later, when the white people arrived in the Northwest, they brought manufactured paints. The Indians began to use these instead of their natural paints. The pole makers were so taken with these brighter colors, that they painted more and more of the totem poles, until the entire surfaces were covered with paint.

The Indians traded with the white men to get
modern tools and paints.

Totem poles were made by professional carvers hired by wealthy members of the tribe. The pole carvers needed not only great skill but great imagination as well. As they were told the story to carve in wood, they had to design the totems so they could be "read" later by the owner of the story. The fact that so many can still be read today is a tribute to the fine work of these Indian wood carvers.

But for every totem pole that can be read today, there is one whose story will never be known. When the pole owner died, his story went to the grave with him. Perhaps you would like to try "reading" the figures on a totem pole. This pole's story is not known, but the pole is real. It was found in the Indian village of Skedans in 1878. We can describe the figures carved on it, but no one has been able to figure out the story they tell. Maybe you can.

The bottom carving is the figure of "Bear Mother," a woman who was changed into a grizzly for mocking the bears. She is holding a small figure—one of her cubs? Above "Bear Mother" is a human head, wearing a high hat. It is similar to the hat Chief Qingi used to save his people from the flood. Remember? Of course, this hat is smaller than Qingi's hat.

The next figure up on the pole is a dogfish whose tongue is sticking out for some reason. (Usually the totem poles show this creature as having sharp teeth.) A tiny human figure is hanging on to the fin of the fish. Many other creatures seem to be riding on the dog-fish's back. There are sea lions next to the human rider. There is also a toothy-mouthed bullhead, and someone is riding on top of it.

The dogfish's tail appears at the very top of the pole. To either side of his tail, is a little watchman in a hat. Were the watchmen there to warn the owner of the house of danger?

It's a beautiful pole, but what magical story does it tell? Have you figured it out?

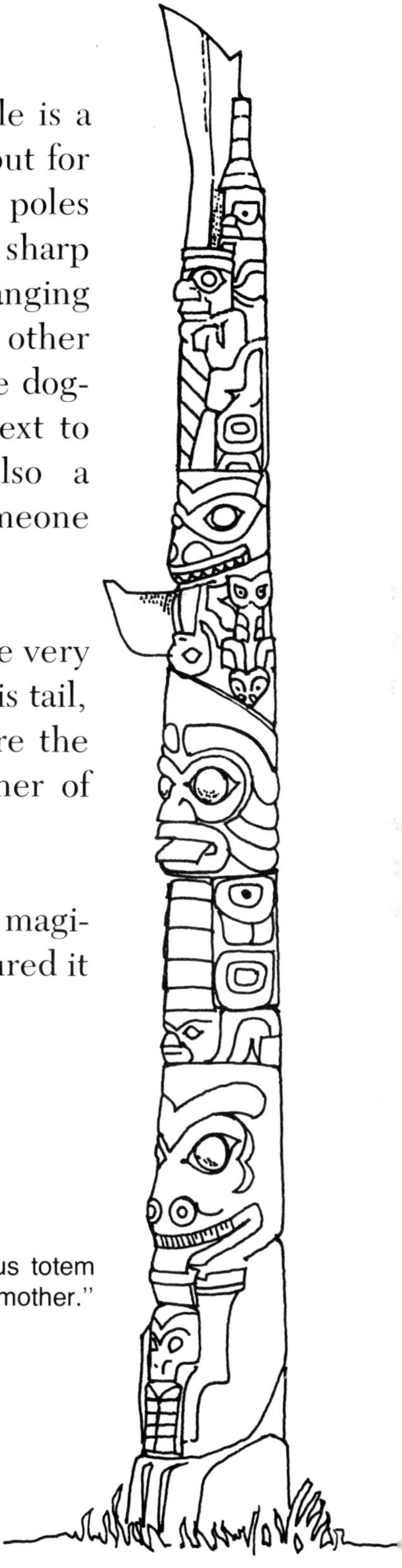

Here is the mysterious totem of the "Bear mother."

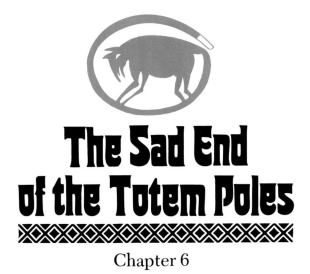

The Sad End of the Totem Poles

Chapter 6

Totem pole carving reached its height in the mid-nineteenth century. Some villages had more than 50 totem poles set in various places. But now almost all the totems are gone from where they once stood. Gone, too, are the villages and the people who lived in them. For many years there have been no new carvings except those made for visiting tourists. The totem poles are a part of the Indian past.

Why did the beautiful, magical totems disappear so completely? The reason is that the Indian culture that produced them died out.

The white man's culture replaced the Indian's. This didn't happen all at once. The earliest Europeans came as traders. They brought with them blankets, kettles, fine steel tools, and door hinges. The Europeans came for furs that they got from the Indians. For their business and their very lives, traders depended on the Indians' good will. The Indians, of course, greatly outnumbered the traders.

Europeans gave something else to the Indians. Along with blankets and metal tools, they also brought the Indians a deadly disease—*smallpox*! Smallpox was unknown to the Indians. Thousands of them died of the dread disease. The Kwakiutl tribe had almost 8,000 people in 1835. Ninety years later, their population was reduced to a little over 1,000. The same horror came to other tribes as well.

There were fewer and fewer Indians, but there were more and more white people in the Northwest. During the 1850s, a gold rush brought swarms of white people. Victoria, British Columbia, had been a small town of 500 white settlers in 1856. Two years later, its population had swelled to 25,000 because of the Fraser gold rush. The gold-hungry invaders were often lawless. They brought whiskey, gambling, and crime

This totem was photographed in British Columbia in 1889.

with them. They had little respect for the rights of the Indians.

Indians left their villages to seek their fortunes in the big boom town, Victoria. No longer was there time for the totem poles and magical stories. Gone were the celebrations and the old customs that were a part of Indian village life.

Many Indians became wealthy during this period. They had been involved in the fur trade since the whites arrived. Now, they provided supplies and labor for the growing fishing industry. Many went to sea and came back with more wealth than they had ever had before.

One temporary result of this new Indian wealth was that potlatches became more and more lavish. Replacing blankets and beads in the 20th century were things like motorboats, stoves, and radios. These were *bigger* potlatches than were ever seen before. They were also the *last* ever seen.

The Indians' wealth began to disappear when the business boom faded in 1929. The potlatch gifts had become too expensive. The gift receivers could not afford to give anything back when hard times came. This was very difficult for the Indians to accept, since it was a disgrace not to give back a more valuable gift. It hurt their pride and ended the potlatches.

Other events, too, helped to end the great Indian way of life. Missionaries had been coming to the Northwest since the early days of the traders. They didn't approve of Indian ceremonies and dances. They thought the Indians were offending God. They hated the totem poles and had many of them chopped down to be burned as firewood.

The Canadian government declared that potlatches and other Indian celebrations were illegal. The message to the Indians was, "Be like us. Follow our ways—or else." So the beautiful totem poles rotted. The wonderful Indian "magic stories" vanished. Indian children no longer learned their old legends and history.

Since the 1960s, many Indian tribes have demanded their political rights. They are trying to reclaim their culture. In the Northwest, Indian

This totem pole was built in front of the Tlingit chief's house.

artists have been studying the native carvings in museums. They are also making copies of their old totems.

Perhaps this means the beginning of a second life for the totem poles. Maybe the magical stories of the young Indians' ancestors will once more be told. Maybe the present-day Indian artists will tell us the tales of Raven and Fog Woman and Qingi's magical hat. Perhaps they will carve us *new* stories of myth, magic, and superstition.

Let's hope so!